CHILDREN IN HISTORY
Romans

Fiona Macdonald

W
FRANKLIN WATTS
LONDON

This edition 2012

First published in 2009 by
Franklin Watts
338 Euston Road
London NW1 3BH

Franklin Watts Australia
Level 17/207 Kent Street
Sydney, NSW 2000

ISBN 978 1 4451 0618 2
Dewey classification: 937

Series editor: Jeremy Smith
Art director: Jonathan Hair
Design: Jane Hawkins
Cover design: Jane Hawkins
Picture research: Diana Morris

Picture credits: Archaeological Museum
Ostia/Gianni Dagli Orti/Art Archive: 2, 6c, 20c.
Archaeological Museum Piraeus/Gianni Dagli
Orti/Art Archive: 26b. Archaeological Museum
Spalato/Alfredo Dagli Orti/Art Archive: 24b, 30ca.
Bridgeman Art Library/Getty Images: 4t, 4b, 13b.
British Museum London: front cover tr, 13t. C M
Dixon/HIP/Topfoto: 22t, 22c. J Doe/Art Directors:
14b. Egyptian Museum Turin/Gianni Dagli Orti/Art
Archive: 26t, 26c. Evgeniapp/Shutterstock: 5. Fiore/
Topfoto: 15. Werner Forman Archive: 20b.
Werner Forman Archive/Topfoto: 24t, 24c.
Mimmo Jodice/Cordice: front cover b.
Vladimir Khirman/Shutterstock: 10c.
Lagui/Shutterstock: 4c. London Art Archive/Alamy:
12b. Araldo de Luca/ Corbis: front cover tc, 19tl, 19tr,
30t. MMM/Shutterstock: 19b. Musée Alésia Alise
Sainte Reine France/Gianni Dagli Orti /Art
Archive: front cover tl, 18c. Musée des Antiquités St
Germain en Laye/Gianni Dagli Orti/Art Archive:
9t, 30b. Musée Archeologique Naples/Alfredo Dagli
Orti /Art Archive: 3, 10t, 10b, 16c. Musée
Archeologique Naples/Gianni Dagli Orti/Art
Archive: 8t, 8b. Musée du Louvre Paris/Marie-Lan
Nguyen/Wikipedia Commons: 9b. Musée du

Louvre Paris/Gianni Dagli Orti/Art Archive: 8c, 12t,
12c, 18t, 18b. Museo Civico Udine/ Gianni Dagli
Orti/Art Archive: 22b. Muzeo Nazionale Terme
Rome/Gianni Dagli Orti /Art Archive: 1, 16t, 16b.
Chepe Nicoli/istockphoto: 28. Gianni Dagli
Orti/Art Archive: 6t, 6b, 20t, 21, 25. Alastair
Rae/Wikipedia Commons: 23. Marco
Scataglini/Alamy: 27. Tomasz zymanski/istockphoto:
17. Tyne & Wear Museums: 7. Roger-iolle/tTopfoto:
14t, 14c, 30cb. World History Archive/Topfoto: 11.

A CIP catalogue record for this book is
available from the British Library

Franklin Watts is a division of
Hachette Children's Books,
an Hachette UK company
www.hachette.co.uk

Printed in China

Contents

Rome: City and People

From around 500-476 BCE, Rome, in Italy, was the most important city in Europe. From small beginnings, it grew into a mighty empire.

▲ According to legend, the city of Rome was founded by twins, Romulus and Remus. The children of a god, they were nursed and brought up by a kindly mother wolf.

From village to empire

Rome began as a cluster of little villages, built on seven hills. Men, women and children worked together to raise sheep and goats, plant vines and olive trees, grow grain and build houses and temples.

At first, Rome was ruled by kings, but in 509 BCE, the citizens drove them out and set up a republic — a state ruled by elected leaders. In 27 BCE, the Republic ended to be replaced by an emperor. A long line of emperors ruled after this.

Rich and poor

There were many different groups in Roman society: rich and poor, nobles and plebeians (ordinary people), freemen and free women, and slaves. Roman children shared the same lifestyles as their parents. Their family background determined their education, career and life-chances.

▼ This stone carving shows a wealthy Roman boy holding his mother's hand.

A growing empire

From around 334 BCE, well-trained Roman armies took control of a vast empire. It lasted until 476 CE, when barbarian invaders conquered Rome. Throughout the Empire, the Romans ruled over people from many different civilisations. In the early days, only people who belonged to families from Rome had full Roman citizenship. After 212 CE, this was given to all people born in the Empire, except slaves.

▲ Many Roman buildings, such as the vast Colosseum in Rome, still survive. Built around 80 CE as a place to hold gladiator fights and other shows, the Colosseum could seat around 50,000 spectators.

ROMAN LEGACY

A long lasting influence

The Romans created a great civilisation, which shaped the cultures of Western Europe and is still powerful today. Many important buildings, such as museums and town halls, still show traces of Roman building styles. European languages contain many Roman words. And this book, like most others, is printed in a typeface based on ancient Roman ways of writing.

A New Baby

Children were important to the Romans. They relied on them to continue the family name, and to work to make money or win fame and glory. But pregnancy and childbirth were dangerous for women and their babies.

Live or die?

As soon as a baby was born, a midwife or slave placed it on the floor and left it for a while. If it cried loudly and kicked strongly, this was a sign that it was tough and healthy, and was likely to survive. If it whimpered, or lay weak and still, the mother or the wet-nurse (a woman paid to breast-feed a baby) might refuse to care for it or feed it.

▼ This stone carving shows a midwife (right) helping a mother (seated) to give birth.

▼ A Roman baby has just been born in this mosaic scene.

One of the family?

Next, the baby was carried from the birth room to meet its father. He, also, had the power to decide its future fate. If he decided to accept the baby, he picked it up and held it. If he did not want the child, he told the midwife or slaves to take it out of his house and leave it on the roadside. The baby might be adopted by a childless couple, found by a slave trader (to raise and sell) — or be left to die.

Choosing a name

Girl babies were named on the eighth day after birth, boys on the ninth. Boys were given a personal name, such as Marcus, followed by the name of their father's family, maybe Julius. They might also have a third name, a nickname, such as Naso (big-nose) or even Brutus (stupid). Girls did not have a personal name; they were known by their father's family name in female form, perhaps Julia or Claudia from Julius and Claudius. Sometimes, the female form of their father's personal name was added. So Julia Marcia was the daughter of Marcus Julius. Where there were several girls in a family, they were numbered: Prima, Secunda (First, Second), or given nicknames, such as Amanda (meaning 'lovable').

▶ This Roman tablet, a slab of stone carved with words, lists popular boys names. The 'V' stands for 'U' in Roman writing.

ROMAN LEGACY

Names

Many Roman names are still popular today, all round the world. For example, Anthony (a family name), Patricia/Patrick (Latin for 'noble'), Placido (Latin for 'peaceful'), Rufus (Latin for 'red-haired'), Serena (Latin for 'calm'), Terence (a family name) and Venus (Roman goddess of love).

Family Values

Once a baby was named, its parents held a party to celebrate the new member of the family. They registered the birth at the Temple of Saturn, and made offerings of thanks to their family's favourite gods.

Working together

Roman families were large, with many aunts, uncles, cousins and other relatives. It was the duty of all family members to help each other, although they sometimes quarrelled. Many families worked together, running farms or businesses, making useful, powerful friends, and sheltering family members who were in need – or in trouble.

▼ A Roman couple hold their newborn baby son in this mosaic.

▲ Roman fathers controlled the lives of their children from birth, as this statue shows.

Paterfamilias

In law, each paterfamilias (male head of the family) had the power of life and death over everyone who lived in his household: his younger brothers, his sons, and all women, children and slaves. He was also responsible for feeding, housing and protecting them. In return, they had to obey him. All younger family members were expected to show respect for their elders.

Tightly controlled

Roman parents had fixed ideas on how to raise a child. As this stone carving reveals, they wrapped new babies in swaddling (strips of cloth) for around 40 days, hoping this would make their limbs grow straight and strong.

▶ Tight swaddling-clothes surround the baby on this stone carving. They are held in place by strips of cloth, or linen cords.

Learning for life

Roman families loved their children, but believed that they needed firm guidance. They thought that each child was born with its own genius (spirit), which gave it character and skills. But the child had to learn to be a good citizen, help their family and serve Rome. So parents taught their children to honour the gods, obey the law and be loyal and hard-working.

◀ This Roman wall painting shows a genius (spirit) with wings.

Rich and Poor

The children of wealthy parents led very different lives to those born of poor parents. In addition, it was difficult for the poorer children to improve themselves and live different lives from their parents.

Easy living

Rich families lived in large houses, with spacious rooms, comfortable furniture, large gardens, and, sometimes, private bathhouses and under-floor heating. They had plenty of food, wore fine clothes and jewellery, and were looked after by slaves. They had money to enjoy art, music and poetry, and to entertain their friends. They were powerful landowners, played a leading part in politics and commanded Roman armies.

▲ A Roman mosaic shows a large family house in the countryside.

▲ This Roman painting shows young children scaring birds away from growing crops.

A struggle to survive

Poor families lived in small country cottages or crowded city apartment blocks. Often, they could not afford to keep their homes in good repair. They had no kitchens or bathrooms — instead, they used public fountains for washing and drinking water, and public lavatories. Their food and clothes were simple, and they had to work hard to grow enough farm produce, or earn enough in their shops and workshops, to survive.

Born a slave

Slaves belonged to their owners. Some were treated badly but others became trusted family friends, and were set free when their owners died. A child of slave parents was a slave from birth, and might be taken away from its parents at any time.

▼ A teenage boy slave, working as a waiter. He is carrying a tray full of food for diners and guests.

Roman tombstones

Roman tombstones can show us how rich families moved around the Empire. For example, sisters Avina and Carina, with their brother, Rufinus, are recorded on their father's tomb in south-west England, though their family originally came from Rome. Little Simplicia Florentina, daughter of a soldier from north Italy, died in York, northern England, when she was only 10 months old.

11

Going to School

Most children in the Roman Empire did not go to school, or learn to read and write. There were no schools in the countryside, only in cities and towns. Schools were open to all, but few ordinary families could afford to pay.

Writing materials

Roman adults and children made notes and wrote short messages on wooden tablets (blocks) covered with a thin layer of wax. They scratched letters in the wax using the pointed tip of a metal stylus, and smoothed away mistakes with the blunt end. Important documents were written with a pen dipped in ink on smoothed, cleaned, animal skin. Books were made by gluing sheets of skin together and winding them round a stick, in a scroll.

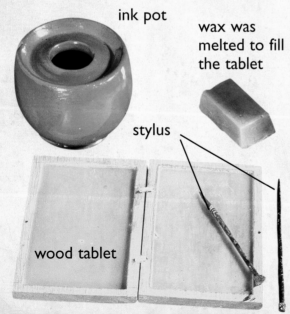

ink pot

wax was melted to fill the tablet

stylus

wood tablet

▲ Roman writing equipment dating from 43 CE, found in York.

▲ A Roman stone carving shows a boy telling his father what he has learnt.

Slave tutors

Some rich families paid for a *paedagogus* (slave tutor) to teach their sons and daughters at home. Tutors and school teachers often came from Greece as the Romans admired Greek civilisation. As well as teaching pupils at home, slave tutors took boys and girls to school, protecting them on the journey and sitting behind them in lessons to make sure that they behaved well and paid attention.

A birthday party invitation

We know that some rich women and girls could read and write, because their letters survive. One – an invitation to a birthday party – was found at Vindolanda, a Roman fort near Hadrian's Wall in northern England. It was written by a scribe, but the sender, Claudia Severa, added a few words in her own handwriting.

▶ Claudia Severa's letter was written on a thin piece of wood. It has survived, in waterlogged ground, for almost 2,000 years.

Private schools

For children lucky enough to go to school, there were two different levels of learning. At elementary schools, pupils aged 7 to 12 were taught reading, writing and simple maths. At grammar schools, pupils aged 12 to 16 studied Greek and Latin language and literature. Girls could go to primary school, but rarely continued studying after the age of 12 – when Roman law said they were old enough to marry.

▼ A teacher (second left) and his pupils around 24 CE. This marble carving was made in Roman-ruled France.

Food and Drink

Like many other features of life in Roman times, the amount and quality of food that children ate depended on whether families were rich or poor. Slaves working in a rich household probably ate better than many poor people.

Unfair shares

Babies were breast-fed for several months, then moved on to bread and milk and other soft, sloppy foods. There were no Roman foods made specially for older children. Historians think that, because men and boys were considered more important than women or girls, they were given more nourishing food, such as meat – and larger portions.

▶ The walls of Roman dining rooms were often decorated with paintings of delicious food.

▲ A snack bar in Pompeii, Italy. The holes in the counter kept wine jars cool. Hot food was sold from the counters.

Meals and snacks

Children ate alongside the other members of their family, at the usual Roman mealtimes. The main meal was in the afternoon, at the end of the working day. Breakfast (before dawn) and lunch were just light snacks of bread and fruit. Families who lived in city flats had no kitchen so they bought food from snack bars and stalls.

14

Favourite tastes

Rich or poor, the Romans liked strong flavours, and many dishes were seasoned with onion, garlic, honey, spices or salty fish sauce. Rich Roman diners enjoyed all kinds of fish and shellfish, roast meat, sausages, little birds and even specially-fattened snails, followed by fresh fruit and pastries. Poorer people made do with bean stew, barley gruel or boiled sheep's head – and lots of bread.

▼ Fish (shown in this Roman mosaic) was popular in main dishes, or sprinkled over anything in the form of fish sauce.

Roman recipes

Several wealthy Romans wrote down collections of their favourite recipes. The most famous recipes are said to be by Apicius, although other writers may have used his name. Roman party dishes were rich, extravagant and rather strange to us; for example, dormice stewed in honey, calves brains with roses, or ostrich with dates and vinegar.

Looking Good

Roman children wore small versions of adult clothes and hairstyles. There were no separate fashions for boys or girls, although they did have special jewellery.

Simple stola

For most of Roman history, women and girls wore a long, loose tunic, called a *stola*. It could be sleeveless or have long sleeves, and was always belted. A woman's stola reached to the floor; a young girl's was knee-length, to give her freedom to run around. Several layers might be worn at once, for warmth, with a *palla* (shawl) or hooded cloak on top.

▼ This teenage Roman girl is pouring perfume into a glass jar. She is wearing a stola, a scarf, bracelets and earrings.

A gold bulla, made for a wealthy Roman boy to wear.

Guard against evil

From birth until 16 years of age – or until a girl was married – children wore a bulla (locket) around their neck, to protect them against evil. The finest lockets were made of gold; poorer children wore a bulla made of leather. Parents and slaves also made jingling necklaces for children out of *crepundia*, little charms, often in the shape of a crescent moon.

Tunic and toga

Men and boys wore knee-length tunics, belted around the waist or, for special occasions, a *toga*. This was a large, flowing, semi-circular cloak, carefully draped around the body. An ordinary toga was white, but senators (senior government advisors) wore togas edged with purple, while boys under 16 wore a toga with a deep crimson border.

◄ Togas were worn draped over the left shoulder, as the Roman mosaic picture shows.

ROMAN LEGACY

Staying healthy

Just was we do today, the Romans eved that sport, swimming, massage and beauty treents could bring well-being. They aimed to have 'a s mind in a healthy body'. So most towns, and many untry houses, had their own bathhouses and exercisms, where men, women and children – at separat es – could keep clean, exercise, relax and care for their and skin.

Fun and Games

In the cradle, Roman babies played with rattles and bells. They may also have cuddled soft blankets. Older children had many kinds of toys to play with and enjoyed sports, too. Children from poor families had to work and had little time to play.

Board games

Gaming boards and counters have been found at many Roman sites. Dice made of clay and ivory have also been discovered. One Roman board game was played like chess, and another like backgammon, but the rules for many others have not survived. Dice were also essential f gambling and guessing contests.

◀ A stone carving, from 86 BCE, shows children playing a game similar to draughts.

▲ Roman counters and dice dating from the 1st century CE.

▲ Some children had small cts to play with, like this one pulled sheep.

Running around

Outside, children played many games, including tag, hide and seek, ball games and blindman's buff. The most popular Roman sports included wrestling, running, jumping and throwing the discus or javelin. Most organised sports were for boys, but girls ran races, danced and took part in gymnastics.

Toys

Little girls played with simple rag doll 'babies'; older girls learned about clothes and hairstyles by dressing delicate dolls made from clay, wax or ivory. Small boys had snapping toy lions, horses on wheels and other model animals.

▼ Roman children had fun playing with moving toys, like this clay horse on wheels.

◄ A Roman doll, from the 2nd Century AD. It has arms and legs that move.

ROMAN LEGACY

Hopscotch

Hopscotch was probably invented by Roman soldiers, some time after 100 CE. It was designed to help them improve their balance when sword-fighting, and to move their feet quickly and nimbly. Over the centuries, the game was copied by soldiers' children.

► Modern-day hopscotch is similar to the Roman version.

Family Prayers

The Romans believed in many different gods and spirits — also in ghosts, demons, witches and monsters. After 313 CE, a new religion, Christianity, spread quickly through the Roman Empire.

Household offerings

As head of the household, a Roman father was chief priest, in charge of family worship. He led the prayers said every day to the Lares (household spirits), the Penates (gods of prosperity), and to the genius (spirit) of the family itself. His wife and children stood beside him. Women and children placed offerings of food or incense on the family altar. On special occasions they decorated it with garlands of leaves or flowers.

▶ The tombstone of a young Roman child.

▲ Little statues of Lares (household spirits) and Penates (gods of prosperity) stand on this Roman family altar.

Ghosts and spirits

Two festivals honoured dead children's spirits. At Lemuria, in mid-May, children's ghosts were believed to haunt their family home. The father walked barefoot through the house at midnight, spitting out black beans, to drive the spirit away. At Parentalia, in mid-February, families held feasts around dead adults' and children's tombs.

► On festival days, prize animals, like this bull, were sacrificed (killed as gifts) to please the gods.

Family festivals

On festival days, Roman families took part in traditional religious ceremonies. Some of these, such as Saturnalia, held in mid-December to celebrate Saturn, an ancient fertility god, were great fun for children. At Saturnalia, all work stopped, everyone wore their best clothes, and joined in religious processions. A child or slave might be chosen as each family's 'king' for the day. Then there was a big feast and everyone played games.

ROMAN LEGACY

Superstitions

Many Roman popular beliefs still survive. For example, Roman people feared werewolves and vampires, and believed that black cats were lucky. However, they thought that left hands and left feet were dangerous. Sinister, the Roman word for left, still means 'scary' or 'threatening' today.

Family Animals

Roman children grew up around many different birds and animals. Some creatures were pets, providing pleasure and companionship. Others were expected to work hard for their living.

Faithful companions

Dogs were the most common family pet. Romans remembered the story of how Romulus, the hero who founded Rome, was rescued and brought up by a wolf. (All dogs are descended from wolves.) Small, white, fluffy dogs, similar to modern Maltese Terriers, were a favourite breed for people living in cities. Bigger, fiercer dogs guarded city or country homes, and helped farmers round up their sheep, goats and cattle.

▲ This very life-like Roman mosaic picture shows a cat catching a bird.

▲ A young Roman child cuddles a – rather large – family dog.

Birds, cats and more

Roman families liked many types of pet bird, from talking crows and singing nightingales to fighting cockerels. They kept pet fish in garden ponds. Cats only arrived in Europe from Africa in the first century CE, but soon became popular, as killers of rats and mice. Among farming families, children had pet chickens, geese, goats, lambs and ponies. It was often the children's task to feed farm livestock and collect eggs.

Roman poem

Part of a poem by Gaius Valerius Catullus, who lived around 84–54 BCE.

My girlfriend's sparrow is dead
She loved him more than her own life.
He was sweet as honey.
He never flew away
But hopped about the house
Chirping to his mistress.
Unhappy day! Poor little sparrow!
My dear girl's eyes are red
and swollen with crying.

Holy signs

Roman children were also taught to think of animals as messengers from the gods. Priests carefully observed flocks of birds flying overhead or the livers of dead, sacrificed animals. They believed both would help them see into the future. In the same way, the Roman army kept holy chickens and offered them food before important battles. If the chickens ate well, this was a good sign. If they refused all food, that foretold disaster!

▲ Romans viewed events such as birds flocking together (above) as signs from the gods.

Growing Up

Roman childhood did not last long. A Roman girl became an adult when she reached the age of 12, and a boy at some time between the age of 14 and 17. Becoming an adult was marked by special ceremonies, new rights and responsibilities.

From boy to man

A boy celebrated his coming-of age on March 17th — the festival of Liber, the god of fertility and freedom. He took off his bulla (see page 16) and solemnly placed it on the family altar, as a gift to the household gods. He changed his childish red-bordered toga for a plain white one, and went in a joyful procession to register his name as a new adult citizen with the government. Then he enjoyed a feast with his family and friends.

▲ A 12-year-old Roman girl shown in a Roman mosaic.

▼ A young student, proudly wearing a white toga and holding a scroll.

Leaving girlhood...

For girls, the end of childhood was marked by marriage or engagement to be married. In law, a girl could marry when she was 12, but many waited until they were at least 15 years old. Marriages were arranged by parents. The girl's family gave a present of money, a dowry, to the boy's family. Girls from poor, ordinary families were more likely to wed for love.

Getting married

The evening before her wedding, a young girl took off her bulla and offered it to the family gods, together with all her clothing and toys. She put on a plain white tunic and yellow hairnet and slept in them, for luck. The next day, she put on a headdress of flowers, plaited her hair and added an orange-coloured veil.

The wedding ceremony was simple: bride and groom linked hands and exchanged promises in front of witnesses. Then the bride's father gave a wedding feast, and finally the bride left for the groom's family house — her new home.

▼ Cupid, the Roman god of romantic love, was often shown as a young child with wings. His bow and arrows shot love straight into people's hearts and led to many a marriage.

ROMAN LEGACY

June weddings

The favourite month for weddings was June because it was sacred to Juno, queen of the gods and protector of women. Being a 'June bride' is still very popular in many parts of Europe today. Roman bridal wear — especially the flower headdress and veil — is still worn. Some people still follow the Roman custom of carrying a bride over the threshold of her new house, in case she stumbles — seen as an unlucky omen.

Not Forgotten

Death and loss of loved ones were part of family life. Although some Romans lived to a healthy old age, others died young, in childbirth, in battle, and from disease or injuries. Half of all Roman babies died before they reached adulthood.

Birth to five

The most dangerous time in any Roman's life was from birth to five years old. Some babies died in their first few weeks of life, from conditions that we can cure today. Others caught deadly infections from polluted water, bad food or filthy streets. Epidemics of measles and other illnesses killed millions. So did diseases such as malaria, carried by mosquitoes.

▶ Peacefully sleeping. This tombstone shows a young, dead, boy, with his pet bird for company.

New risks, old remedies

Older children were also at risk from disease. As boys and girls grew bigger and became more adventurous, they were more likely to die in playtime accidents, such as falling out of trees. Young married girls often died during pregnancy or childbirth. Roman doctors and women healers tried to cure patients with simple operations and herbal remedies. Parents also said prayers and made offerings to the gods.

◀ A doctor (right) examines a sick woman. Hygeia, the goddess of health, stands behind him.

Roman poem

Part of a poem about a dead child by Marcus Valerius Martialis, who lived around 40–103 CE.

She was my dear and my delight

She died just six days before she was six years old.

Now let her run, to play among friends,

Let her speak, to whisper my name.

Soft grass, hide her fragile bones!

Earth, cover her gently! She trod so lightly on you.

Saying goodbye

Funerals and tombs were very important to the Romans. They were a way of saying goodbye to dead family members – and of staying in touch with them. The dead person was carried to the cemetery in a procession with music and chanting. Bodies were cremated and placed in urns, or buried in shared family tombs that lined the roads leading away from towns and cities. People visited tombs often, to pray and to 'feed' the spirits of the dead with milk and wine.

▼ Roman tombs have survived in the ancient Roman town of Ostia in Italy.

27

Activities

Why not experience some of the things that Roman children did, by trying some of these activities?

An easy Roman recipe

Try this simple dessert. You can leave out the pepper and the cinnamon if you like, but both were popular Roman spices. Serve with stewed, dried apricots or fresh grapes – favourite Roman fruits.

For each person:

- 50g–75 g thick yoghurt or fromage frais
- 15 ml runny honey
- tiny pinch of ground black pepper
- big pinch of ground cinnamon

1. Heap the yogurt or fromage frais on to a dish and stir in the pepper.
2. Drizzle honey over it.
3. Sprinkle cereal on top for a twist on this Roman recipe.

How to wear a Toga

A toga was a very big, very heavy, woollen cloak, shaped like half a circle. Roman men and boys asked a slave or a friend to help them put it on.

1. Ask your helper to stand behind you, holding the toga with the straight edge at the top.

2. Pull about one-third of the toga over the front of your left shoulder. Let the left point of the toga reach your knees. Support the weight of the toga with your left arm, bent at the elbow.

3. Ask your helper to pass the rest of your toga across your back and under your right arm.

4. Pull the right point of the toga across your chest, and over your left shoulder.

5. Ask your friend to pull the right point down past your waist at the back.

6. Take a few steps. If the toga is draped around you in a balanced way, it should stay on.

Speak like a Roman

The Romans spoke Latin, the language of central Italy. Roman children learned Latin from their parents, nursemaids or slaves.

salve! = Hello   *vale!* = Goodbye!

salvete amici = Hello friends!

licetne mihi = Please (may I)?

tibi gratias ago! = Thank you!

bene facis! = Well done! (or Thanks!)

puer = boy	*puella* = girl
mater = mother	*pater* = father
infans = baby	*frater* = brother
soror = sister	*cena* = dinner
domus = house	*canis* = dog
feles = cat	*avis* = bird
ubi? = where?	*quando?* = when?
bonus = good	*malus* = bad
minus = less	*plus* = more

Write numbers like a Roman

Roman numerals, or numbers, appear on some clocks and watches.

I = 1	II = 2	III = 3
IV = 4	V = 5	VI = 6
VII = 7	VIII = 8	IX = 9
X = 10	XI = 11	XII = 12

Make crepundia (charms)

NOTE: these are for children over 7 years old, NOT FOR BABIES.

You will need:

- Card, about 10 cm x 10 cm
- Stick-on metal foil OR metallic paints and brushes
- Pen or pencil, scissors, hole-punch
- Gold, silver or glittery string or fine ribbon
- Stick-on plastic jewels, or sequins and glue (optional)
- 3 little bells

1. Draw a crescent moon shape on the card. Cut it out.

2. Cover the crescent on both sides with foil or paint. If painted, leave it to dry.

3. Make a hole at each end of the crescent, and three holes in the middle of the longer side.

4. Thread string or ribbon through the end holes, so that you can wear the crescent like a necklace.

5. Fasten the little bells to the longer side of the crescent. Let them hang loosely, so they can jingle.

6. If you like, decorate one side of the crescent with plastic jewels or sequins.

Timeline

c. 1000 BCE First settlement – a farmers' village – at Rome.

753 BC According to legend, the city of Rome is founded by Romulus and Remus.

c. 753–509 BCE Rome is ruled by kings.

509 BCE End of Roman kingdom and start of the Republic.

334–264 BCE Romans win control of all Italy.

47–44 BCE Army commander, Julius Caesar, takes power, but is murdered and civil war begins.

27 BCE End of the Roman Republic. Army commander, Augustus, becomes the first Roman Emperor.

c. 30 CE Jesus is executed in Roman-ruled Judea (now Israel, Jordan and Palestine). A new religion, Christianity, begins, but Christians are persecuted.

43 CE Romans invade and conquer southern Britain.

79 CE Vesuvius, a volcano, erupts in southern Italy; this buries the Roman seaside town of Pompeii in larva.

117 CE The Roman Empire reaches its largest size.

313 CE Christians are allowed to worship freely; soon Christianity becomes the official religion of the Empire.

324 CE Emperor Constantine founds a new capital city in the East: Constantinople (now Istanbul).

395 CE The Roman Empire is divided into East and West.

410 CE Visigoths (warrior tribes from the north) attack Rome. The Romans leave Britain.

455 CE Rome is wrecked and looted by Vandals (warrior tribes from the east).

476 CE The last emperor in Rome is overthrown. The end of the western Roman Empire. The eastern Roman Empire continues, with a new name: Byzantium.

Glossary and further Information

barbarian the name the Romans gave to warrior tribes that lived outside their Empire.

BCE/CE BC stands for 'before Christian era'/CE stands for 'Christian era', referring to the birth of Jesus Christ in 1 CE.

bulla a locket worn by children. It contained protective charms.

citizenship rights given to someone who belongs fully to a country or nation.

cremated when a dead body is burned to ashes, which are then scattered or buried.

crepundia little jingling charms strung into a necklace. The Romans thought they brought good luck to their children.

crimson deep red.

epidemics diseases that spread quickly to many people.

emperors lone, strong-man rulers.

genius spirit.

gruel a food, like soup, made of grain and water cooked together.

legend a story handed down from the past

Lares household spirits.

malaria a disease that causes a high fever, and which is spread by mosquitoes.

mosaic a picture made up of tiny pieces of coloured stone, glass or pebbles. The Romans used mosaics to decorate floors.

noble a person born into a powerful and wealthy family.

paedagogus slave tutor.

paterfamilias father of a family.

Roman Empire the countries ruled from Rome, including much of Europe, Egypt and some of the Middle East.

stola long, loose tunic worn by women.

stylus a pointed stick used for writing on wax tablets.

Further information

There are many museums and websites you can visit to find out more about Roman children. Local museums often run events about life in Roman times.

www.bbc.co.uk/schools/romans/families.shtml
A helpful summary of Roman family life, with interactive features.

www.museumoflondon.org.uk/English/Learning/Learningonline/features
Find out about life in Roman London from this museum website.

www.pbs.org/empires/romans/empire/family.html
This webpage is about Roman marriage. Follow the links for further information about life in Roman times.

http://rome.mrdonn.org/index.html
A very helpful website about ancient Rome.

Index